Magical Math

A book for young children and their parents

To my children, who taught me how thinking is accomplished. — J.G.

ISBN 978-0-9987100-0-6

Printed in the United States of America

Vision Academy Publishing

visionacademypublishing.com

TABLE OF CONTENTS

Counting and Combining
The Hidden Bean Game - 6
The Shoe Game - 10
Build Like An Elf! - 14
The Ten Pair Game - 18
The Lucky Clover Game - 22
Pixie Races - 26

Multiplication/Division/Fractions
A Pretty Pebble Picture - 30
What's In A Number? - 34
Mystery Rod Game - 39
Dwarf-in-a-Box -43

Logic
The Unicorn Game - 46
The Troll Game - 49
The Fairy Ring Game - 52

Geometry
Dragon Games - 58
        Which Make Triangles?
        Which Make Squares?
        Magic Circles
        Playing around with Perimeter and Area
Naiads, Dryads, and Symmetry - 68

Introduction

Just like magic, math goes beyond our everyday experience, taking us into new realms where anything can happen. Though the proofs of these mathematical fantasies are far out of reach for young children, exploring simple but profound math concepts in a light-hearted way can awaken their desire to know more. It is this desire that can bring big dividends when it's time to learn the more difficult parts of math.

Math for young children is typically focused on solving arithmetic problems. But arithmetic is just one small part of the fascinating field of number theory, and number theory is just a small area of the vast subject of mathematics. Introducing children to the more interesting parts of math at an early age expands the scope of what they have to think about in quiet moments, which is when learning is internalized.

And thinking, not the accumulation of facts, is the goal of math education. In a day when calculators are everywhere, we must focus on the essence of mathematics: thinking through a complex scenario, pulling out the right facts, and applying logic to them. As G.K. Chesterson said, "It isn't that they cannot see the solution. It is that they cannot see the problem." Encouraging children to explore open-ended math questions can help them become creative and unintimidated when approaching new math topics. Unfortunately, as a society we have come to believe that cramming arithmetic facts into children's heads at ever-younger ages leads to success in math. It may indeed lead to higher test scores in the short term, but "memorize-test-forget" takes the place of true understanding and internalization of useful and useable knowledge.

So let's get rid of math "tunnel vision" and replace it with a focus on nurturing broad and flexible thinking skills. The math facts will then grow naturally out of the logic and number sense that the child has acquired, and the tests will take care of themselves.

This book introduces children to various math concepts by engaging their imagination and encouraging free exploration and play. The illustrated pages are meant to be read to the child, simplifying vocabulary and instructions if necessary for the youngest ones. The first few games are simple enough for most four-year-olds, and as the book advances the activities require more thinking skills; the final ones are meant for kids close to age eight. Sprinkled throughout are parent pages with additional information on the activity plus background knowledge on why it can be useful. These pages are to help you as a parent understand what it takes to guide your child in developing thinking skills.

On with the show!

The Hidden Bean Game

It may surprise you to learn that all sorts of magical creatures love to play with math. Dwarves and elves, fairies and griffins, each one has a favorite game that they play. Why do they love math? Because math is magical. It lives in the Land of Imagination. Sure, we use math in every-day life, but that is usually the less magical parts. Some math is dull and tame, but some is fascinating, like the difference between a cow and a unicorn. As you start on your math journey, remember that even though learning is fun, sometimes it isn't easy. But if you stay excited about it, you may catch a glimpse of the unicorn.

Fairies also live in the magical Land of Imagination. When they are very young, fairies like to play a game with tiny magic beans that you will also enjoy if you are very young. They gather a few, and then one of them hides them and the others go looking for them. As they find the magic beans they call out how many they have collected, and then arrange

them in pretty patterns on a leaf. They see that five beans on a leaf makes very different patterns than four or six beans. Even though they sometimes argue about it (fairies can be very quarrelsome) they usually decide that seven is the most mysterious number, eight makes lots of pretty patterns, but nine is their favorite. Which do you like best?

Another favorite game fairies play with magical beans is to put five or ten of them under a leaf. Then one fairie pulls out a few and says, "I have three beans in my hand. How many are still under the leaf?" The other little fairies guess, and then they look under the leaf and see if they were right. Pretty soon they have to use more and more beans or the game gets boring.

And in case you wonder, sometimes they hide the beans so well that they cannot find them. By the next day the lost beans have grown into magical beanstalks which lead the fairies on new adventures.

one-to-one correspondence

Playing around with beans may not seem like doing "real math." But noticing patterns is crucial to math development, and should be emphasized right from the beginning, far more than learning number names and symbols (numerals). The names and symbols are human conventions—shortcuts that have developed over time to communicate with others about quantity. Don't start there. Or if your child has already picked this up, deemphasize it. Let the child gradually build up her own sense of what numbers are about by playing with physical objects and involving as many of her five senses as possible (yes, you can use jelly beans for this activity).

One-to-one correspondence is where small minds begin developing numeracy. The famous child development researcher Jean Piaget defined this as "representational thought," which develops in toddlers as they begin to understand that one thing (a word, a picture) can represent another thing. One-to-one correspondence is also how the human race began to use numbers: to our ancestors, one pebble in a pouch designated one sheep in the field; twenty-seven pebbles in a pouch represented twenty-seven sheep. So if you have one extra pebble that you don't have a sheep for, you'd better go looking for it.

The hiding and pattern activities listed here are a great place to start playing with numbers. Engaging curiosity and interest is essential for kicking the brain into learning mode. Talking about fairies gets the creative juices flowing in a way that boring symbols and facts do not. So while pretending to be fairies, place five beans on a table and then scoop them up between your two hands, closing your fists around them so they are hidden and your child is not sure how many are in each hand. Then open one hand and say (for example), "I have three beans in this hand. How many are in the other hand?" Have your child think about this, and if she's having any difficulty, put five more beans on the table for her to use to assist her thinking, as she separates them into two piles accordingly.

Now let her have a turn trying to stump you with the same question, hiding the beans between her two hands. When you think she's ready, try the game with ten beans. Why five and ten? That goes back to why we have the number system that we do: because those numbers are what we have always at hand (or hands). If a child develops a rock-solid sense of which numbers make up five and ten, she will be able to rely on that understanding all throughout arithmetic and beyond.

When these seem to be fully learned, try putting five beans in one hand and six in the other. Help your child see that she should still make a ten with the five and five, but will have one left over. Let her call the beans "ten-one" as this is consistent with what she understands and will start her off on a solid path to understanding our base-ten number system. "Ten-two, ten-three, ten-four…" should be emphasized rather than twelve, thirteen, fourteen. Then "two-ten-one, two-ten-two, two-ten-three," etc. for twenty-one, twenty-two, twenty-three. Of course, she will have heard the standard counting numbers, and of course you can point out that these are the same, but "These names are the 'easy counting' names, so they are what what we're going to use for a while."

Keep adding beans or other counters to your game as you play in short sessions over time. Keep focusing on creating tens out of the counters, grouping the tens together and stacking the others in a separate pile to the right.

Why are you doing this? To build up an intuitive sense of how our number system works, before it is ever overtly taught. Eventually you'll transition back to the traditional names by explaining that "-teen means ten" and "-ty means ten: twen-TY means two tens, thir-TY means three tens, for-TY means four tens," etc. But the discussion of the frivolous question of what we call numbers can wait until the understanding of how they work is secure.

> **Our minds are much more powerful when discovering than when memorizing, not least of all because discovering is much more fun.**
> *John Holt*

The Shoe Game

You may have heard of house-elves, or Brownies, as they like to be called. They are cute little people just a few inches tall who live in homes in Scotland. Though they are sometimes mischievous, they like to do small chores around the house in exchange for gifts of food.

One of the things they like to do is to arrange the shoes that children have left carelessly lying about. They gather up all the shoes they can find and then make matches with them and put them away. If they cannot find a match for a shoe, they occasionally lose their temper and make the house a bigger mess than it was in the beginning—normally they love order and hate messes. So if you are ever in Scotland, please make sure your shoes stay together in pairs. And leave a few cookies sitting out from time to time.

Be a Brownie! Get a laundry basket and go around your house collecting shoes. Now dump them into a pile, count them, and then match up the pairs. If every shoe has a match—even if the shoes aren't the same, but each one has a "friend"—then that number is an even number. If one of the shoes doesn't have a "friend," that number is an odd number.

EVEN = they each have a friend, ODD = one of them doesn't have a friend.

Now get out a die and look carefully at it, noticing the patterns of dots. Which numbers on the die are even? Odd? Why?

Roll two dice and arrange that many shoes into a pattern that helps you understand the number. Is it odd or even?

You will find that the Brownies set a good example for you. Cleaning up and organizing are skills you will use every day in your home and also in your math. Messy math isn't magical!

Grouping numbers

Children learn to string numbers together in the counting sequence by hearing it over and over in everyday life. What they should also begin to hear at an early age is the skip counting sequence: "2, 4, 6, 8" (you can add "Who do we appreciate?!" if it makes you happy). Anything that makes pairs can be used to skip count. Look at the legs on a person, a dog, an ant, a spider, a centipede—most living creatures have a bilateral body plan.

As soon as a child has fully grasped counting by ones, he should be gently discouraged from relying on it exclusively. Simple counting leaves him liable for mistakes as he misses or double-counts an object. Instead of counting a random group of things, help him arrange the items into pairs and use skip counting. If the items cannot be moved (like when counting objects in a picture) help him visualize pairs of objects within the group.

Creating order out of chaos is one of the main cognitive functions of math. And using different strategies for different occasions keeps his thinking flexible. I've known older children who, when approaching a group of objects clearly grouped into twos or threes, still insist on counting each one even though they know the multiples of two and three. They're in a rut, which keeps them in the "slow and error-prone" camp. Again, let your child first become secure in counting by ones, then introduce skip counting.

If you think your child is mature enough, you may want to begin listing odd and even numbers in columns or rows on paper or a dry erase board. This will begin training the brain to recognize that every member of that set (row or column) has something in common: in this case, oddness or evenness. This skill will eventually transfer over to understanding how addition and multiplication charts work, and much more.

"Messy math isn't magical!" Helping your child create order, like matching objects by different attributes as he cleans up his toys or his sock drawer, is more than just a life skill, as important as that may be. These activities also help him create a logical, orderly brain (this takes longer for some kids than for others!).

Game extensions

Roll two dice and think about what happens when you put an even and an even together to make one number. Would that number always be even? What about an even and an odd? And what happens when you roll an odd and an odd? Write a rule for this.

Add Up is another game that aids in creating a need for thinking about odds and evens. Give each player a small handful of dice and choose a number within the range of what the dice could add up to. Let the players choose how many dice to roll (maybe three if your number is 14, but you could roll four or five), and have a contest to see who can roll that number the fastest. Players can set aside dice that have been rolled to a number they like, and keep rolling the rest until they all add up to the target, but they must stick with the number of dice they started with—they can't just use three to make the target number if they began rolling four.

This game builds on the understanding of even and odd numbers, as the players will see that if the target is 14 and they roll two numbers that are odd, the third dice must be rolled to an even number. Also, fairly soon you should notice that your child is beginning to estimate how many dice would give him the best chance of quickly rolling the target. Estimation is now seen by many math education experts as the key skill to be learned in elementary school math, and children should be given ample opportunity to estimate in their daily lives—in work and in play.

> **Play is often talked about as if it were a relief from serious learning.**
> **But for children play is serious learning.**
> **Play is really the work of childhood.**
>
> *Fred Rogers*

Build like an elf!

In the magical world some of the most wonderful creatures are the elves. Not to be confused with your Elf on the Shelf, elves are human-sized, never grow old, and are very beautiful. Elves love to build things, and different types of elves love to build different things. Wood-elves build boats and castles, homes filled with lovely furniture, and weapons of war to defend their cities from the goblins. Santa's elves are a tribe of wood-elves who went to live at the North Pole to build toys because they enjoy that so much (and, yes, they are rather short—they are about as tall as you).

Elves are very clever, and they enjoy using their hands to show how smart they are. Sometimes they also use magic, but not until after they know how to build that thing with their hands using real tools. This is how they make sure that all their magical contraptions will really work.

Show that you have a good brain too as you become a creative builder. Build big things with blocks of all sorts. Make repeating patterns of colors. Grab a friend and each of you make a drawing of something interesting (animals and insects, trees and flowers, trains and spaceships) then exchange drawings and build what you see.

Now get some number rods and start building numbers from one all the way up as far as you can go. What is the simplest way to make a number? What is a more complicated way?

Create beautiful patterns. Make a spiral starting with your smallest rod then going out from the center, using longer rods as you go. Make a staircase, either lying down or standing up. Now before you put them away, be sure to

make a stair pattern that shows which of the
rods goes with which other rod to make ten, in
preparation for the next activity!

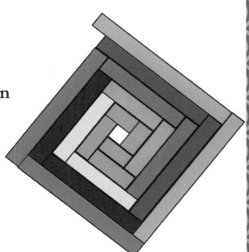

STAGES OF DEVELOPMENT

Educators today recognize that children need to understand the truth behind number symbols before they begin working with them very much. Otherwise they won't have a good basis in reality and will do ridiculous, impossible things with numbers and not even know that they are breaking immutable natural laws.

We know from extensive research that number sense develops gradually, resulting from exposure to numbers in a wide variety of contexts and activities that are meaningful to the child. The development of number sense occurs in three recognizable stages. Young children do not have the ability to think abstractly. Their brains are making connections at a furious pace, but in the early years they need to be able to use as many of their five senses as possible to assist their thinking. Concrete objects—manipulatives like sticks, blocks, or beans—are vital to developing strong number sense.

The second stage of math development is the mental image stage, in which children are able to picture things in their mind and manipulate them there. They are gaining a feel for how large each number is relative to the others, and getting to know what tricks it plays (like the fact that nine things can be arranged into a square, while ten cannot).

After further brain development, the image is no longer needed, and purely abstract thought can be easily used. They can use the number nine in their head to do different tasks, can chop it up, put it back together, multiply it, etc., all without reference to any internal or external image.

Since young children have yet to develop the parts of their brain needed to process symbols and abstractions, pushing them to manipulate numbers symbolically can cause them to become math-phobic. The solution is to first spend a lot of time physically playing with numbers: building models with manipulatives.

Number rods are the *sine qua non* of math education. There are several types, but we've always preferred those that do not have markings on them and do not have connectors on the ends—those interfere with the play aspect of the rods and make them only useful for doing math, which is not what we're going for. Present the rods to your child with a little build-up—maybe wrapped as a gift—and spend some parent/child time making pretty patterns or interesting gadgets. Playing with the rods will cause your child to discover their properties in a more organic and meaningful way than if you "teach" them to your child. Since they are one centimeter units, have a centimeter ruler on hand to lay them next to for checking the sums.

in mathematical thinking

Another hands-on activity that helps kids think about numbers is to create a number zipline. String beads on a cord and tie it between two chairs so that the beads can slide back and forth. Put on nine beads, then use a different kind of bead—maybe a fat wooden one so that you can write the number "10" on it if you wish. Then nine more beads and another fat one with "20" on it, etc. This can help your child learn to count by fives and tens, and you can use it for various things like tallying the score of a game.

Our base ten number system is an abstract and difficult concept for many children, which is why "thinking with objects" is the ideal for young children. When you can see that your child is beginning to think about this (are they trying to write or talk about big numbers?) purchase a base ten number kit for him. There's simply nothing else like it for getting a good grasp of how our number system works, and you can use it to solidify thinking about borrowing/carrying/regrouping when that becomes important.

> **Too often, our (math) books lead us to give the child an abstraction, then we must spend great energy and creativity trying to explain the meaning of the abstraction. If we persevere long enough and if the child's mind is mature enough, we can succeed in this, but how much better it would be if children arrive at meaning with the raw materials of arithmetic, with objects and number lines and Cuisenaire rods, with checkers and game scores and batting averages. When enough meaning is built, an abstraction can follow.**
>
> *Ruth Beechick*

THE TEN PAIR GAME

Deep in the ocean the merpeople spend their days happily frolicking, playing hide and seek with octopuses and tag with dolphins. They love to play games with shells, and one of their favorites is the Ten Pair game. Merpeople have ten fingers like us (though they don't have ten toes!) so they use a base ten number system like we do, building their numbers up on each set of ten. Little mermaids and merboys play the Ten Pair game so that they can easily add and subtract big numbers because they are never confused about which numbers go together to make ten.

Each merperson who wants to play finds twelve scallop shells and on the inside writes the numbers zero through ten; the last shell is left blank. They gather their shells into a pile, and then take turns flipping one over and placing it in the center. If that shell makes a "ten pair" with another one in the center (for example a three is flipped over and a seven was already there) the player may collect them for his point pile. Or if there is a "ten pair" that the other players haven't noticed, he can collect that one on his turn. When the blank "wild" shell is flipped, the player can use it with any other shell but must say which number it represents. Whoever has collected the most shells at the end of the game wins.

What does the winning merperson receive as a prize? Why, any pearls that were found that day on the search for scallop shells!

Try playing the Ten Pair game, and you will see that soon you can add and subtract numbers bigger and smaller than ten as easy as breathing... under water...if you're a mermaid.

GROWING THE MENTAL TOOLBOX

As noted on the previous parent page, mental math isn't easy for young children, and they shouldn't be pushed into it. However, as they grow and begin to feel comfortable discarding their manipulatives—which children naturally do as soon as their mental toolbox is sufficiently developed—you should be prepared to assist them in making the transition.

One hint is to encourage them, when adding two numbers, to avoid simply counting them all, but instead, do "counting on," as follows: The child is adding five plus eight. She says "Eight" out loud while holding up five fingers. Then while saying "Nine, ten, eleven, twelve, thirteen," she puts the fingers down one at a time. This method cuts down the amount of counting the child does, which decreases the chance for her to make a mistake or to have her attention be zapped in "Squirrel!"-like fashion.

This, of course, just helps ease through a temporary stage in the development of thinking about numbers. A more permanent tool is found by learning the number pairs that make up ten. The reason this game is so valuable is that once the pairs that make up ten are fixed in the brain, they can be used in many ways. Instead of using any form of counting for five plus eight, the child would know that eight always goes with two to make ten, so she breaks up the five into a two and a three, sticks the two onto the eight to make a ten, has three left over, so she knows she has thirteen, or "ten-three."

The Ten Pair games works well with two to four players—card images can be downloaded at visionacademypublishing.com. Any cards left over at the end of the game can be discarded, or your child can state the matching number to claim the card.

Game extensions
Have players match three cards, instead of just two, to make a ten. You may want to add more "wild shells" into the game so the players can figure out a number that they want to use to make a match.

This can also be played like Memory, with all cards turned face down and each player trying to find ten-pairs. Or like Go Fish, with the cards shuffled randomly and five of them dealt out to each player. Players hold their cards in their hand and ask if a neighbor has a certain card with which they can make a ten-pair. If they do not, the player chooses one from the remaining cards stacked in the middle. If it makes a match, he puts it in his point pile. The player with the most matches at the end of the game wins.

For kids more advanced in math, you can do a Twenty- or a Thirty-Pair game. Or make cards with all the factors of a number (choose one like 48 that has a lot of factors) and the goal is to find two cards that multiply up to that number.

If your child seems to like this type of thing, play some simple dice games. A very flexible one is Bull's Eye. Pick a number according to the math skills of your child, as low as 10 or high as 100. Roll two dice and take either the sum, the difference, or the product. This number is written down and added or subtracted to any previous numbers to try to hit the target. For example, if your target is 20, and the child's previous rolls have him at 16, and then he rolls a 2 and a 3, he could choose the sum of 5, the difference of 1, or the product of 6 to add to his number. If he goes over the 20 target, on the next turn he'll try to hit the target on the way down by subtracting. The first player to hit the target is the winner.

Each problem that I solved became a rule which served afterwards to solve other problems.
Rene Descartes

The Lucky Clover Game

Leprechauns love money, especially gold coins, which they find underground as they're building new tunnels for their homes in Ireland. They also love trickery, and though rumor has it that they put a pot of gold at the end of a rainbow, you will never be able to find it so don't bother trying. However, you may be more successful if, while visiting Ireland, you set some leprechaun traps near the openings to their underground homes. If you catch a leprechaun, he must, by Leprechaun Law, grant you three wishes, and that could be great fun!

You can play a game very popular with leprechauns. Get some coins— gold would be great, but if you don't have any gold coins lying around, silver or copper work as well—and get some three-leaf clovers. Write three numbers that add up to ten on each of the clover leaves, putting one number on each leaflet (writing on real leaves is difficult for anyone except Leprechauns—you may want to use paper). Then give each player an equal number of clovers upside down in a stack, and the same number of coins as clovers.

On their turn, the player picks up a clover, looks at the three numbers, covers one with a coin, and then places it in the center of all the players. The first player to correctly guess what number is under the coin gets to keep the coin, and the player who has the most coins at the end of the game wins. Is his prize that he gets to keep the coins? You decide.

THEORIES OF LEARNING

There is a "sweet spot" in math, as in anything else. It must be challenging enough to encourage thought, but not so challenging that it invites failure. Russian psychologist Lev Vygotsky called this the Zone of Proximal Development (ZPD): what you are ready to learn but don't yet know. Each person is completely unique in his brain development and in what he has experienced in his life; thus each of us has our own ZPD for each area of our lives. Classroom teachers must, by default, teach to the average understanding among their students, but Vygotsky recognized that this has very little value, even for the children whose understanding of a subject is within the range of the instruction being offered in the lesson. In fact, he said, "Practical experience … shows that direct teaching of concepts is impossible and fruitless. A teacher who tries to do this usually accomplishes nothing but empty verbalism, a parrot-like repetition of words by the child, simulating a knowledge of the corresponding concepts but actually covering up a vacuum."

So if learning doesn't happen in the classroom, through direct instruction, how does it happen? It happens in quiet moments, when what you've heard or seen or done is connected to what you already know, to physically build and expand the brain's neural network supporting that piece of knowledge. Sometimes known as the brain-mind cycle of reflection, "first-person learning" occurs when we ponder on our own experiences and intuitions. It's the process that causes one to really own the knowledge, making it useable for guiding further decisions and solving future problems.

But as noted by many psychologists and educational researchers, schools are not set up to facilitate first-person learning, but rather second-person (learning from "you") or third-person (learning from "them"). Unless the child voluntarily chooses to reflect on and internalize what has been presented, memorization takes the place of understanding, and the gains are superficial and temporary. In the Albert Einstein quote here he distinguishes between first-person learning as "fantasy," and second/third-person learning as "absorbing positive knowledge," and states that the former has been much more valuable overall. Elsewhere he said, "Imagination is more important than knowledge. For knowledge is limited, whereas imagination embraces the entire world."

In order to make progress in our understanding of how people learn, we need to be careful of how we use the word "student" and completely eradicate the word "pupil" from our vocabulary. Instead, we should refer to those seeking understanding of something new as "learners." A learner is someone who is actively participating in an educational pursuit, one that he's chosen for some reason. The reasons for learning are everything from a love of the subject down to fear of punishment for not knowing it (grades are an example of this). Obviously, the things that you learn because you enjoy them are going to be those that you reflect on in quiet moments, those that become true first-person learning and make a permanent impact on the brain.

So what is the takeaway for the average parent? Understanding how the brain works empowers you to take charge of your child's education, even if he's in school. You can find ways to lessen the pressure on your child to learn something that he's clearly not ready for. You can dovetail the topic he's studying with a project at home that he's actually interested in that uses that particular math skill (a game, a hands-on project, cooking, etc.). Whenever your kids are designing, building, crafting, or sewing they are using math. They are thinking about measuring, aspect ratios, perspective, and center of mass in general ways that lay the groundwork for real understanding when these topics are covered formally. Whenever you do a project, if possible, involve your kids in the planning and math stages: "How much paint do we need to buy to paint your room?" etc.

The Lucky Clover game can obviously be used with more complicated math, like the Ten Pair game, and additionally you may want to make some lucky four-leaf clovers and write four numbers on them that add up to your target number. Perhaps you can use nickels on those instead of pennies to sweeten the prize.

> **When I examine myself and my methods of thought**
> **I come to the conclusion that the gift of fantasy**
> **has meant more to me than my talent for absorbing**
> **positive knowledge.**
> *Albert Einstein*

Pixie Races

If you go walking through the wild moors of Cornwall, where the Land of Imagination is often to be found, don't be surprised if you occasionally hear tiny, tinkling laughter coming from over the next hill. When you get there, of course, there will be nothing unusual to see, but be assured that you have just disturbed a pixie party. Pixies are tiny, child-like creatures who are very merry and love to play games. They also love the animal creatures that are small like themselves, and frequently use them in their games.

Their favorite game is something they call "Hobgoblin," but it is really a lot like tag. The pixies first began by racing all kinds of creatures, but they soon found that the tinier ones would always lose to the bigger, faster ones. Since they are tiny themselves, they were sympathetic to this, and came up with the following game:

A line is drawn in the dirt and marked with stones at regular intervals. The tiny pixies mount up on ants, crickets, grasshoppers, frogs, bunnies,

and birds. One pixie shouts out a number and the first animal jumps forward that many stones. Then he shouts another number, and the next animal jumps forward, and then the next, and if one animal lands on a stone that is already occupied, his pixie rider tags that animal out of the game.

The trick is that the ant, being the smallest can only walk from one stone to the next, but the bigger animals can jump twice or thrice what the ant can do, and even more. So if an ant gets a "three" he will go forward three stones, but if a cricket gets a three, since he can jump to the second stone, he can go ahead six stones. On any turn, though, the animal can reverse directions, and instead take his jumps back toward the start. So there is strategy and math involved in figuring out which direction the pixie should have his mount jump. But luckily the pixies like math and are good at it.

Can you gather some friends and play "Hobgoblin" too?

PLAY = LEARNING

The **Pixie Race** game scoops up essentially all of traditional early-elementary math and turns it into a party that your child will want to attend. First you need a number line: a yardstick or plastic tape measure works great, or draw one on a dry erase board or a long strip of paper. How long you make it will depend on your child's math ability—0 to 60 is reasonable for children who are starting to have some number sense, but it could be shorter for shorter people, and could go into the negative numbers if you want to introduce that.

You will need a die and small pictures of an ant, a cricket, a grasshopper, a frog, a rabbit, and a bird (which can be downloaded and printed from visionacademypublishing.com) and some way of attaching the pictures to your number line of choice: magnets, clothespins, plasti-tack or tape.

Game: Players can decide which animal to be, and depending on the number of players, may choose to be more than one, alternating turns with each animal.

The ant cannot jump, he just crawls down the number line one number at a time, to the right and left (positive and negative, adding and subtracting).
The cricket makes short hops of 2.
The grasshopper can hop 3's.
The frog does "4" jumps.
The rabbit can jump 5's.
The bird, with the help of his wings, can do leaps of 10. (You may want to leave out the bird and the rabbit for younger kids.)

When the die is rolled, the player can:
- Add: move their piece ahead as many spaces as the number on the die
- Subtract: move their piece backward that many spaces
- Multiply: jump their piece by its value that many times. For example, if they have the grasshopper piece, which moves in three jumps, and the roll is four, they can jump four times, so move ahead OR backward twelve spaces.

If your roll would take you off either end of your racetrack, you can move or jump to the end and then reverse directions to complete the turn.

When one animal lands on another animal at the end of his turn, he tags that animal out and it must be removed. The last creature on the path wins.

In the event that the game is going on too long and the players' attention spans are short, you can say, "We'll each take three more turns, and whoever is closest to (whatever number is at the center of your racetrack—20 on a track of 40) is the winner."

You can also tell stories: "The ant was walking down a path one day. He went to the 1, then the 2, then the 3. 'Excuse me please,' said the frog as he jumped over the ant (to the 4) and then kept going. Then the ant crawled to the 4, but the cricket wanted to get going (from the 2) so he had to wait until the ant crawled to the 5, so he could jump to the 4, then the 6." Etc. Use your imagination—then have your child tell you a story. It's estimated that people remember about 20% of what others say, but about 80% of what they themselves say. So encourage your child to describe and elaborate upon the activities you're doing with her.

Make sure that your child notices the patterns made when each animal jumps: the cricket and frog only land on odd numbers if they begin on an odd number, but the grasshopper and rabbit land on an even, then an odd, then an even while they are jumping. The rabbit and the bird make a related pattern that should be noticed as well. Focus on beginning multiplication as repeated addition: "The cricket hopped two TIMES and got to four."

> **All play is associated with intense thought activity and rapid intellectual growth. The highest form of research is essentially play.**
> *N.V. Scarfe*

a Pretty Pebble Picture

If you've seen many paintings of fauns, magical creatures that are half man and half goat, you may have noticed that they are often painted holding a flute of some sort. That's because fauns love music. They love to play songs and dance with other creatures in the light of the full moon.

You probably knew that, but did you know that music is filled with math? Put on a piece of music that a faun might have played, and you may hear the rhythm say "1, 2, 3, 1, 2, 3..." or you may hear "1, 2, 3, 4, 1, 2, 3, 4...". These are patterns in time that are repeated over and over. You will also hear musical patterns in the tunes fauns play as their fingers move around on the flute, making different sounds. The notes are intervals between one pitch and another one. You'll hear step intervals when the music goes from one note to the next, skips when the music goes from the first to the third note, jumps when the tune goes up to the fourth note, leaps when it goes to the fifth, etc. Try this on a piano, xylophone, or recorder.

If you've noticed all this, it won't surprise you to learn that fauns love to play with the spaces or intervals between numbers. They draw a chart in the sand that contains the counting numbers—small charts for little fauns, big charts for big fauns. Then using different colored pebbles they take turns placing a pebble on each number that is on the "interval chain" of a smaller number: first they do skips all over their chart, then jumps, then leaps, and so on as far as they wish to go.

They like to see which numbers are on the most chains and what is the highest number on their chart that isn't on any chain, They think about why the pebbles make the patterns that they do. But mostly they just enjoy looking at the pretty, colorful patterns.

finding and making patterns

The ancients viewed the world through a lens much different than ours in many ways, especially regarding education. Instead of adults holding children captive, making them listen to and and regurgitate what they said, the children would instead follow the adults around: watching them, imitating them through play, trying to gain adult skills because of their internal motivation to do so.

When they entered their teens it was time for a formal education, if one could be had at that time and place and economic level. In our modern worldview we think that children must be formally schooled from an early age or they'll grow up to be dunces, so waiting this long to study seems like lunacy. But the ancients knew that children would have spent those early years playing and helping with tasks around the house or farm, and would have naturally picked up all the "soft skills," plus the academic basics, on their own. This alowed them to jump right in at an advanced level for their formal studies.

The ancient Greeks thought it essential to gain skill at grammar, logic, and rhetoric—the trivium—first. Then the youth launched into a study of arithmetic (pure number), geometry (number in space), music (number in time), and astronomy (number in space and time)—the quadrivium.

Today many view music as a non-academic pursuit, but again this goes counter to ancient thought, it being one of the four advanced subjects. Music deals with intervals in time and pitch—it's all about patterns. If your child is already playing a musical instrument, hooray! His life will be blessed by his musical abilities, and multiple studies have shown that musical training improves IQ (Miendlarzewska and Trost. 2013).

As your child grows he will naturally encounter number intervals and multiplication, and should be encouraged to own it—it's just repeated addition after all. Schoolish math pounds away at addition and subtraction *ad nauseum* for years, such that when multiplication and division are introduced they are quite a shock to the system. It doesn't have to be this way if all four concepts are introduced more or less simultaneously, though very gently, as in the Pixie Race game in which the child is finding the multiples of a number by making ever larger interval jumps. But at the first, slightest hint that the child is beginning to use math beyond what he's comfortable with, you should pull out the number rods and let him use them.

The pattern activity is an important one, and much can be learned from it to lay a solid foundation for a child's number sense. Make a large, poster-size chart of the numbers 0 to 99. You can do 1 to 100 if you wish, but there are distinct cognitive advantages for an early learner in a chart that shows 0 through 9 on one row, 10 through 19 on the next, and so on. You can do 0 to 109 if that makes you happy. But with young children you'd only want to use the top 30 or so at first.

Now have your child take colored counters (bingo chips, buttons, etc.) and designate the first color the "2 color"—let's say it's red. Have him place a red marker on all the multiples of 2 (all the even numbers). Now have him pick a color for 3—let's say yellow—and put that on the 3 and "all the numbers that are three more than the last number: 1, 2, put one down, 1, 2, put one down…".

Before going on, have him look for a pattern, both in the matching up of the "2 color" and "3 color" markers (the red will be together with the yellow on the 6, then alone on 9, then together on 12) and also in the large patterns they create (red will be all in straight rows, yellow will be a scatter pattern).

Then, since 4 is already marked with red, move on to 5, and mark all those multiples in another color. Then 7, then 11, etc. When you've gone as far as you can go, you'll see that you've found all the prime numbers—they're the first number of each color, on each number chain.

You can do a similar thing with addition and multiplication charts, finding patterns and marking them with colored counters. Whenever you think they're ready. There's no rush.

A mathematician, like a painter or poet, is a maker of patterns. If his patterns are more permanent than theirs, it is because they are made with ideas.
G. H. Hardy

What's in a number?

Griffins have been known since ancient times and are found in the art and stories of civilizations throughout the world, from Egypt to Rome, from India to England. They are generally thought to be large beasts with the head, wings, and legs of an eagle, while the hind legs, body, and tail are those of a lion. Sometimes they are shown with four lion legs, other times they may have the tail of a serpent.

But the real differences between griffins are told in stories that go beyond appearances to get at the true nature of the beasts. It is said that there are actually three species of griffins.

Gryffins are friendly and intelligent, though they sometimes play tricks on you.

Gryffens are slovenly creatures who don't like to be awakened more than once a week.

But the gryffons are the ones you don't want to meet—they are proud, dangerous, and do NOT like humans!

Just like griffins, the real nature of numbers lies beyond what the symbols look like. Numbers have personalities too, and as you get to know them they can become your friends. Some numbers, like eight and nine, don't look too different when you write the symbols (8 and 9), but when you take a closer look, you will see that they are as different as gryffens and gryffons.

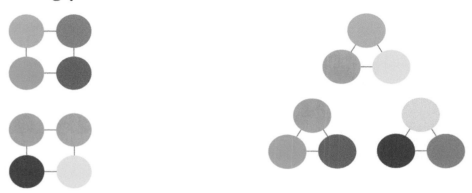

Get eight marshmallows, gumdrops, or grapes and join them together with spaghetti noodles, toothpicks, or bamboo skewers into a **3D** shape. Then try the same thing with nine marshmallows—what can you do with that?

Now get eight sticks and join them together with as many marshmallows as you need to make a closed shape (eat any extra marshmallows you don't need—just to be tidy). Then make nine sticks into a **3D** shape— it should be a pretty one, so take a picture of it and send it to your grandma.
What shape can you make with six sticks and four marshmallows?

You should start to see that numbers are made up of different groups of other numbers. These are the factors of a number, which help give the number its personality.

Now get some factor cards, and play the game that your parent will teach you. Look for patterns on the cards, because these patterns are the ones that really matter when you are thinking about numbers.

making math meaningful

Much of what passes for math education is just empty exercises in recall of unrelated facts. The tests we give children demand that they cough up the desired answer to an arithmetic problem in order to get a good grade. But if we want math to be meaningful to our kids, it needs to paint a picture. Patterns should be revealed, and beauty and usefulness uncovered. There must be coherence and a feeling of "this is all going somewhere." It's analogous to teaching a pre-reader a list of randomly selected sight words that cannot be used together for anything meaningful, versus working through a simple but elegant book filled with meter and rhyme, finding patterns that transform the words into music (*The Cat in the Hat* comes to mind).

We must get rid of the schoolish mentality that the reason for learning is to prep for a test. How do we do this? By helping our children make connections. When a child finds a pattern in numbers, it can be very powerful, both for recall of the matter at hand and for the attitude with which he approaches future math topics.

So get rid of the random. If you want your child to practice arithmetic facts, work on them as "fact families": 3+5=8, 5+3=8, 8-3=5, 8-5=3. Model all of this with number rods—subtraction with number rods is accomplished by laying the rod to be subtracted next to the rod to subtract from, and then filling in the gap with whatever rod fits.

Or focus on adding one number to a whole string of other numbers—make a number rod staircase of 1+2, 2+2, 3+2, 4+2, etc.

But a step above this type of approach is helping your child get acquainted with the number itself. Is it odd or even? A prime or composite number? If composite, what are its factors? Is it a square, triangle, or cube number? As your child grows you can introduce her to some of the many simple sequences, like Fibonacci or Lucas or Perfect numbers. Where does your number show up in Pascal's triangle? Explore what the number would look like in other number bases or systems: binary, hexadecimal, Roman, Egyptian (see Index for resources).

Back on a more simple level, you may want to just focus on one number until your child has really made friends with it. Have a "Number Safari" month in which you spend a day or two pointing out a certain number wherever you see it: in a group of objects, a pattern in a painting, the spots on a butterfly's wing. Look for the symbol in large numbers and small ones and in fractions, on street signs and at the grocery store. Make numbers with different art media and line them up in a Number Zoo.

Here is a game to play along with these other activities: **What's In A Number?**© Purchase or make a set of factor cards (see visionacademypublishing.com).

Deal six cards to each player (2 - 4 players is best). Place one card face up in the center of the players and put the rest of the cards face-down in a "draw pile" stack next to it. The players may look at their cards, but then each must place the cards face-down in a row in front of him.

The object of the game is to play all the cards in front of you and empty your "hand." The youngest player goes first, and flips over any of his six cards. If the card shares a factor with the face-up card in the center of the table, he may place it on top of that card. If the player's card doesn't share a factor with the card on the table, he turns the card back over and must draw another card from the stack in the center, look at it, and place it face-down next to the other six.

Example: A 15 card could match with a 5, 10, or 20 card, OR it could match with any card showing a factor of 3: 3, 6, 9, 12, etc.

Exception: Any prime (2, 3, 5, 7, 9, 11, 13, 17, 19, 21, 23) can be placed on any other prime, since they share the factor of 1. But sharing the factor of 1 is only allowable for the primes. The composite numbers 8 and 9 aren't a match since the only factor they share is 1. The prime 3 and composite 4 aren't a match, but 3 and 21 are a match since 3 is a factor of 21 (there are triangles in 21).

Give it a try, and you will see that the kids are scanning the cards for the factors and doing a lot of thinking about composite and prime numbers.

Note: Though stories of griffins have been told throughout world cultures for thousands of years, the story that I took the three species of griffins from was just written in 1957: *David and the Phoenix,* by Edward Ormondroyd. It's high up on my list of the most charming children's books ever written.

Beauty in mathematics is seeing the truth without effort.
George Polya

---

mystery Rod Game

If you ever meet an elf while hiking in the Mystical Mountains, he will probably be traveling: going somewhere or returning home from somewhere else. In either case, he'll probably have a bag slung over his shoulder, since that is the fashion with mountain elves. If you ask him what is in his bag, he won't want to tell you, and you'll never know if it was something boring like bread, or something amazing like enchanted flowers. Or something in between like bread made from enchanted flowers.

But you can comfort yourself by playing a mysterious elf game. Two games, actually; the first is very simple, and the next is very silly.

Get some number rods and put half of them in a sack and hand them to the player who is being the elf. The rest of the rods are available to the other players. One player holds up (for example) a brown rod and asks the elf, "This is eight units—find a rod in the bag that is half of eight." Or, "This is eight units—can you make a rod that is twice that long?" If he can, then he passes the bag to the next player.

If the players are a bit more advanced, you can say, "This is ten units—find a rod that is one tenth of this length." Or "Here is a six rod. Can you show me what number four of these would make?"

Later you can move it up to "This brown rod now represents one unit. Find a rod that is one fourth of a unit."

Now for some silliness: Put the bag on the floor and at least five players (the more the merrier) form a circle around it. The game leader picks a rods and, turning to the player on the left (let's call him #1), says (for example), "This is a nine."

Player #1 must then say "A what?" and the game leader says "A nine" and hands the nine rod to him.

Player #1 then turns to the player on his left (#2) and says "This is a nine." Player #2 must then say, "A what?" but Player #1 cannot answer the question and must turn to the game leader and say, "A what?" and then the game leader says, "A nine," which #1 repeats back to #2 and hands him the rod. That rod continues to travel around the circle <u>clockwise</u>, with each player unable to answer the "A what?" question until the game leader has confirmed that, yes indeed, it is still a nine. It continues to travel until it has been successfully returned to the game leader.

BUT MEANWHILE… after the game leader hands off the nine rod to player #1, he turns to the player on his right and shows (for example) a three rod, saying, "This is one third of a nine" and then it travels around the circle <u>counter-clockwise</u> following the same pattern as the other rod. Hilarity ensues when the rods meet in the middle and cross paths. No one will EVER again forget that three is one third of nine.

CHILDREN AND GAMES

Speaking of fun, there is a delicate balance between playing a game with a child and coercing a child into an activity that he has not chosen. The spark of interest a child initially shows toward anything new is quickly extinguished whenever he senses that the activity is mandatory. People like to be free, and far too many children are turned off to learning by being forced to participate in things they have no interest in.

Games can break down a child's resistance, if he's developed one, to learning. Granted, some people like games more than others, but anyone can enjoy a game if two things are present: interesting objects or illustrations that make us want to join the story (all good games are really stories on some level), and a living person that we want to spend time with—of which, the latter is far more important. We model the attitudes that we want our children to obtain, so your child should see you approach new activities with interest and joy.

When presenting a game or activity to a child, you should choose a good moment: tummy is full, had enough sleep, quiet relaxed atmosphere. Do some build-up, like it's going to be great, but don't go crazy since there's a chance it won't take (if your child isn't ready for it) and you want him to believe you the next time as well.

Then allow your child to play with the game objects like toys for a while—to get this out of his system and allow him to focus when you teach how to play the game. That could take just moments, or it could be an entire play session in itself—you may want to hold off teaching the game until the next time you pull out the objects, after he's familiar with them.

Don't underestimate the vast undertaking, for a small child, that it is to learn to play a game, and thus the amount that can be learned from doing so. On top of the usual sitting and paying attention—difficult enough for some children—he is being asked to learn what all the objects in the game are for, what he can and cannot do with them, and how to combine these things to work toward an end. He often needs to come up with an offense and a defense, and this is in addition to just being able to do the thing the game is asking you to do if it's a word game, a number game, or a game based on another skill. This is really putting the brain to work, so watch your child and find a way to wrap it up quickly if he's reaching his limit. Several short sessions are often better than one longer one.

Children need what we rarely give them in school—time for "Messing About" with reading—before they start trying to learn to read, to make the connections between letters and sounds. They need time to build up in their minds, without hurry, without pressure, a sense of what words look like, before they start trying to memorize particular words.

In the same way, they need time for "Messing About" with numbers and numerals....They need to build up a mental model of the territory before they start trying to talk about it.

We teachers like to think that we can transplant our own mental models into the minds of children by means of explanations. It can't be done.

John Holt

Dwarf-in-a-Box

When Snow White found seven dwarves living in a house deep in the woods, she was very surprised, and rightly so. Though the seven dwarves did spend their days digging for riches in a mine, living in a house is unusual for dwarves. Most dwarves live in the mines that they dig, only occasionally venturing out to trade their gold for food and clothing. Why do they live in mines? Simply because they enjoy it. They love feeling safe and secure with solid stone all around them.

As you can imagine though, sometimes living in a mine can be a bit cramped. Having enough space to swing a pickaxe can be tricky when a new excavation is begun, so dwarves have become very good at fractions. At first just one dwarf will work in a small cavern, but as he chisels away at the walls, soon it's big enough for two dwarves to work in. So they draw a line down the middle dividing it into two equal spaces, to be sure they don't hit each other with their shovels and picks as they work. When the cavern is bigger, they divide it into three parts and let a third dwarf in. And so on, until the space is divided into many small areas in which the dwarves can safely work away at finding gold, silver, and precious jewels.

To make sure that the young dwarves understand fractions, the dwarves pound gold into thin sheets and cut it into fraction shapes. Then they see which ones will fit together inside the whole shape. And when they get good at it, they compete at a game of chance, racing to fill their box with fraction shapes that fit together just right. Only when they can win this game do the dwarf elders allow them to start swinging pickaxes in close quarters with other dwarves. Safety first!

VISUALIZING DIVISION

The concept that "the larger the denominator, the smaller the piece" often really confuses kids when it is formally introduced around the age of eight. This is one case in which earlier really is better: young children can understand fractions just fine as long as they are presented as real objects that are sliced and diced into ever smaller pieces. So you just draw a horizontal line on a paper and say, "That line means chop it!" and you chop an apple. "How many pieces is the apple chopped into?" Write a two under the line and say "That is how we show how many pieces a thing is chopped into."

Then you hand the child a piece and say, "How much of the apple do you have?" "You have one of the two pieces." Write a one over the line. "That is how we show when we have this much of an apple."

Then put the apple back together. "Now how much of the apple do we have?" Change the numbers to $\frac{2}{2}$ (always show fractions vertically, not horizontally in the beginning). "If the apple is chopped into two pieces, and we have both pieces, then we have the whole apple—see for yourself! If we write the same number on the top and the bottom of the chop line, then we have one whole thing."

Now chop it again and play around with changing the numbers respectively to fourths, adding and subtracting the fourths, talking about how $\frac{2}{4}$ is exactly the same thing as $\frac{1}{2}$. Keep it short. Eat the apple when you're done. Maria Montessori and Charlotte Mason and Dr. Peter Gray would all be proud of you: a lesson which is hands-on, short, and playful.

Note: At our house we call halves "two-ths" for a little while in the beginning of fraction time, simply because it's consistent with fourths, fifths, etc. But as the kids are already familiar with the word "half," we transition quickly to that, with the excuse that "two-ths" sounds too much like "tooths," which is not even the correct plural of "tooth," so we say "half" and "halves" instead.

Another concept that causes great confusion is understanding that fractions are...*drum roll*... THE SAME THING as division. Fairly soon after showing how we write fractions, you

$$4 \div 2 \qquad 4/2 \qquad 2\overline{)4} \qquad \frac{4}{2}$$

could mention that there are (at least) four different ways we show numbers being chopped up:

"If I have four halves of an apple, I have two apples. (demonstrate) These are all the ways you can write it. You can say 'Four chopped into two groups, four divided by two, or four⟩ halves'—it's the same thing."

It can help kids to remember which number gets chopped if you say the division bracket is a "table, and the four is hiding under the table so it won't get chopped up—but it will be found and chopped—and will be served in pieces on top of the table." (Or maybe don't say that—if you have very sensitive children.)

To play Dwarf-in-a-Box, make seven squares (at least six inches across) of different-colored cardstock or foam sheets. Cut each squares into a fraction: halves, thirds, fourths, sixths, eighths, ninths, and leave one whole. You can mark them with the fraction name, or leave them blank so the child must think about how much of the whole square they each represent.

Make a set of these for each person – or make the game more cut-throat by only having one set – but you at least need the whole square for each player to build on.

Get some beans and write the fractions on them with a marker (lima beans are good for chubby fingers) Write ½ on two beans, 1/3 on three beans, 1/4 on four beans, etc. Put them in a non-transparent cup.

Shake the cup then let a player draw a bean (without looking), pick that fraction from the pile of foam fractions, and put it on his cardstock square. Each player tries to fit together fractions to make a whole. At any point in the game if he's having trouble fitting his fractions together, a player can elect to use a turn to return a fraction from his sheet into the pile. The first person to make a perfect square, with no overlaps or gaps, is the winner.

Alternately you could use a spinner marked with the fractions. Or use a die (the number rolled is the denominator of the fraction – the 1 on the die could represent 1/8th, and the 5 could be 1/9th). But this makes the game harder, because of the probabilities involved.

> **That which is desirable on its own account and for the sake of knowing it is more of the nature of Wisdom than that which is desirable on account of its results.**
>
> *Aristotle*

The unicorn Game

Unicorns are one of the most beautiful creatures in the magical world, but they are also very mysterious. You may have a fuzzy stuffed unicorn that you sleep with that is all pink and purple and sparkles, but a real unicorn is a very difficult creature to get to know. That is because they are very solitary and shy, seeking out places in the world where no one else is near. They enjoy silence, and feel safe only in the company of trees and wildflowers. If they sense someone coming—whether man or beast—they are gone in a flash. For such a beautiful creature, they camouflage very well. Good luck finding one.

But you may enjoy a few unicorn games. For the first one, play the unicorn game as a unicorn would—solo. Get a 64-square chessboard and some small pictures of unicorns to use as tokens. Start placing them on the board, but be aware that since unicorns are shy, you cannot place them next to each other. All the squares in a loop around each unicorn must be empty (including diagonals). But you want to have a big herd of unicorns, so how can you place the most unicorns possible on the board without crowding them?

Now that you have a feel for how this game works, try playing against an opponent. While taking turns, one player places light unicorns only on light squares, and the other places dark unicorns on dark squares. Your goal? Create a unicorn herd larger than your opponent's.

How to win? Look for patterns. Find ways to place your unicorns that block out a space for you to place another unicorn, but that don't allow your opponent to put one down also.

The Troll Game:

I'm afraid at this point that I must tell you about some unpleasant creatures who live in the Land of Imagination. Some of them never learned to "treat others the way you want to be treated," and they have really bad manners. They are greedy and selfish, they are unkind and unwise, and they don't respect other people's property or their lives.

Trolls are an example of this unpleasant sort. They do all the nasty things just mentioned, and to top it off, they never brush their teeth, so they have very bad breath. When they growl, "Who's that tromping over my bridge?" it's not so much the voice that scares you. It's the smell! They do not have pink hair that sticks straight up, and they never, ever smile.

"Who Gets the Last Scrap of Food"

So what do they do when they're not trying to eat billy goats or capture princesses? Hanging around their caves between hunting trips gets boring, so they've made up a game called "Who Gets the Last Scrap of Food." It's an ugly name, so feel free to make up a nicer one for it, but this is how it's played:

Make three piles of items: you can use food—small crackers work fine—or small toys, blocks, or counters of some sort. Put just a few items in each pile—maybe 3, 5, and 7. On his turn each player removes as many items as he wishes from <u>just one</u> of the piles. The person who removes the last item wins.

You may want to try a variation in which the players build the piles at the beginning of the game by taking turns placing two items in one of the three piles. This can go on until they are both satisfied with the pile sizes, but each pile will have an even number of blocks in it. Now play as usual and see if things come out differently.

BRain DeVeLOPMeNT

The unicorn game and the troll game are both adaptations of simple games that have been around for a very long time. The reason they are so durable is, I believe, for that very reason: they are simple enough that a small child can play, yet can stump an adult. They cause you to feel, while playing, that if you just applied some brain power, you'd see how to create a winning situation for yourself. So you power up those neurons and you think! And that's the real goal.

When children begin playing games, they only focus on what is a good move to make in the moment. But soon they see that thinking like that won't help you win—in many games you have to plan ahead a bit. It's generally a truism that when a child can easily think ahead to the next step in her game strategy, she is ready to take on math problems that add a second step, like mentally adding two digit numbers. When she can think ahead to the third move that she will make after the current one, her logic and memory skills are advanced enough to tackle fairly complex math.

The unicorn game ties in closely with visual-spatial intelligence as well as logical-mathematical. It's easy for some children but challenging for others to see the loops around each unicorn that is placed, to look for spots on the board where they can place another one, and ultimately to plan out how to reserve a spot for their last unicorn so they can win. So that's where the growth in thinking can occur: applying those two types of intelligence together.

The troll game is purely logical-mathematical thinking, but is such a linear game with so few distractions that children immediately begin to realize that the only way to win it IS to think ahead a few steps. Some will find this easy and some difficult, but either way it's a good exercise in maintaining focus and making your mind to go down a path for a while. Logical thinking skills usually take a big jump ahead around age eight, so if it's not clicking for a five-year-old, put it aside and try it again in a year or two.

But note that even if your five-year-old is "too young" for an activity or game, it can still be valuable. There are many theories of learning and intelligence (the Theory of Multiple Intelligences referred to above is one), but a basic principle is that you have to have thought about something in general before you can think about it in specifics. By the time a child is three, the neurons in his brain have connected to each other in about one quadrillion synapses, a truly mind-boggling number, and actually many more than the brain needs. The synapses that are used to carry messages (i.e., what he is experiencing through his five senses plus his own internal ponderings) are strengthened; unused synapses are gradually eliminated through a pruning process that lasts until the early twenties. Intelligence grows as neural pathways through the brain are created, linking together important pieces of stored information.

A mature brain is a combination of nature and nurture, of biology and lived experiences. Each person has his own level of understanding in each subject depending on a multitude of factors that go back to infancy. Parents are in the best position to assist their child in learning since they know his personality, his past experiences, his likes and dislikes. It still can be difficult to predict which activities will really spark his interest, but in providing gentle exposure to a variety of learning activities, you are helping him prepare his brain for more advanced information processing. Vague thinking about a topic must precede precise thinking.

This is why mixed-age learning environments are so valuable. A young child in the vicinity of two older children engaged in an activity may not look like he's paying attention, but he's likely picking up many clues about what they are doing and beginning to think in general ways about it. These thoughts are creating real, physical connections in his brain which are necessary as he approaches the ability to do the activity. We may say he's getting more mature, but really the difference between a child who can and one who cannot engage in an activity is that exposure to the activity (and others like it) has created biofunctional changes in his brain that permit him to now participate in the activity.

So introduction to a new field of knowledge must be done gradually. The first time you play the troll game, you will likely not get it either, but as you play you should rapidly feel those blank spots in your knowledge filling in.

> **Your job is to provide the spark and the fuel, not the fire itself. Present pursuits to your child in a way that elicits her voluntary interest. Instead of forcing your child to acquire improvements for the sake of purposes that are not yet her own, you inspire her to develop her own purposes by sparking her interest in something new. Then you fuel the flame that you sparked…. Your role is to inspire ends, not to impose means.**
>
> *Dan Sanchez*

The Fairy Ring Game

Sometimes while walking in the woods you may find a beautiful circle of mushrooms known as a fairy ring. They are not really uncommon, since the real mushroom "plant" lives under the ground and grows these cute little hats around its edges to spread its "seeds." But seeing one is still exciting, because legends tell us that fairies come out to play in the moonlight in and around fairy rings.

What is less well-known is what games they play within these rings. One is similar to leapfrog; another is a form of dodge ball using dandelion tops. But their favorite activity involves stringing strands of spider web between the mushrooms. Then they perform formal fairy dances along the strands, twirling and bowing gracefully as they go.

Sometimes while doing their dances, the fairies are a bit flustered to find that if they start a dance on a certain mushroom they always end up back at that same mushroom without visiting all of them. In other fairy rings, with different numbers of mushrooms, the same dance will take them to every mushroom before they come back to their starting point. As they are not mathematically minded, they haven't been able to figure out why that happens. Which is sad, because if they understood math, they would be able to choose the right dance for each fairy ring.

But you can figure it out! Make a circle of dots—let's say eight dots to begin with. Now choose which "dance" to do—you may want to go around the circle drawing lines connecting every second dot. What happens? Do you get to every dot in the two dance? Now try a three dance on the same fairy ring, just skipping to every third dot. Did you get to every dot? How about connecting every fourth dot? What happens when you connect every fifth dot in a circle of eight dots—which one of the patterns does this look like?

Now try a circle with a different number of dots. Keep all your fairy rings with all your dances, and compare them. Do you see a pattern forming? Patterns are very important in math.

Can you help the fairies know which dance to do in a ring of twelve mushrooms to get to every one?

DEVELOPING PROBLEM-SOLVING SKILLS

The fairy ring activity is another one that can be done at multiple levels, from very simple to fairly complex. Depending on your child's age and interest, this could be a quick, very hands-on activity with putting blobs of playdough on your table and stringing yarn between them as your child's fairy doll dances or as his truck drives along the strands. Our favorite is to use dry erase markers—they work great on windows and smooth floor tiles as well as dry erase boards. Draw circles of dots and then connect the dots into various star shapes by jumping over different numbers of dots.

The question should quickly become apparent: why can't I get to every "mushroom" in a circle of eight when I am skipping every other mushroom, but in a circle of nine I do get to every one by skipping? What if I skip to the third dot? The answer may require making a chart of which "dances" touch every dot in which circles and then pulling out your 100 number chart marked with the factors of the numbers.

But how does one know to make a chart, or even think about the circles in connection with factors? How do we even begin to problem-solve when we've never seen this type of problem before? The key lies in learning to think about thinking itself: metacognition. This includes things like defining or categorizing problems before attempting to solve them; conscientiously avoiding oversimplification, analyzing our biases, and weighing all the evidence; and not becoming so emotionally attached to the answer that we came up with that we spend a lot of energy defending it even when it is wrong. Whenever we can step outside ourselves, analyzing the strengths and weaknesses of our own thinking, and suggest improvements to ourselves, we are in the world of metacognition.

Young children, of course, might be able to peep through the window into this world, but certainly cannot yet walk through the door. But we as parents can assist, by modeling it: "Hmm, the fairies found a ring of twelve mushrooms, and I don't know which dance they should do to get to each one. But as I look back at the other circles we just did, it seems like something is going on with the even and odd numbers. I'm going to think about that some more. What do you think about that?"

The development of metacognition is helped along by verbalizing what we are thinking. When we put thoughts into words, and even better, into writing, which is "words that stay," it is far easier to hold our ideas up to the light and scrutinize them. If the thoughts remain only inside our head, they can skitter away into the darkness if we come looking for them.

Japanese math teachers know this. They create a classroom culture in which interesting problems are worked on and discussed in small and large group formats. They spend much more class time examining much far fewer problems than in a typical American classroom. What are they doing during that time? Coming up with unique methods of solving the problems and, whether right or wrong, talking to other students about them.

A summary of one study comparing U.S. and Japanese methods of math education states:

> Math lessons begin slowly and build methodically in an attempt to engage students in a challenging problem. Japanese teachers place a much greater emphasis on thinking about the problem than on quickly coming up with a solution. Students are directed to work in small groups on one or two problems. At the elementary level, students use mathematics kits that contain visual aids and manipulatives. These are considered important elements in representing and discussing mathematical solutions.

Whether you love or hate the Japanese educational system, their math test scores do beat the U.S. scores consistently and by quite a margin, so they're doing something right!

Besides modeling metacognition by talking about our thought processes, what else can we do to encourage our children to begin thinking about thinking? Looking for patterns in math is important, but when we have found one, we need to step back and remind ourselves that the pattern might be leading us down the right road, but we shouldn't oversimplify things—the pattern may break down later on. We shouldn't burden small folks with too much detail, but if we see that they're understanding where a pattern leads, we may want to plant a "What if…" in the back of their minds.

Here are some more hints to foster metacognition and build problem-solving skills:

- Begin early asking the simple question: what happens next? "What happens next if you hit your brother? What happens next if you move that checker to that space?" Work backwards: "Look at these holes that have been dug in our flower bed. How do you think they got there?"
- Provide many opportunities for comparing, sorting, and classifying objects in the home: puzzles and blocks are some obvious physical ones, but you can also talk about art and music, personalities and behaviors in these ways.
- Teach brainstorming: "What are five things you could do if someone is picking on you at the playground?" "What are some things you could use to help you multiply 1 ½ x 2 ¼ ?" (get out the measuring cups, use number rods or fraction rods, draw a diagram)
- Emphasize creative methods rather than application of memorized steps—the thinking

55

process, rather than the solution, correct or incorrect: "I like how you thought about the multiples of 5 when you wanted to know the difference between 30 and 55."

- Don't say, "What is THE answer?" Say, "How many ways can you make this number sentence true?" Foster the desire to experiment with a problem by asking open-ended questions that help the child see the problem in a new light. Then help your child go through each method he came up with and decide which ones arrived at the right place.

- When your child is confused about how to do an operation, have him substitute simple numbers for the complex ones. "OK, let's think about this. If you had to divide two apples between six people..." This takes him back from Abstract thinking into Mental Image mode, where he is more comfortable. If you need to go all the way to Concrete mode, go ahead and pull out the number rods and let him discover the process. When he has refreshed his memory of the principle of the operation, he can apply this to the more complicated problem.

- If your child is very stumped, but still interested (not frustrated or upset), show the process with a different problem, and let him apply that insight to the one he's working on.

- If he does get upset, put the math away with a "don't worry about it for now" statement, and make sure he understands that his value in your eyes has nothing to do with his ability to do math.

Sometimes we are, unknowingly, looking at our world in a fuzzy manner. Mathematical thinking allows us to see our world in a sharper way, where details that were once hidden now come into focus, and the beauty and structure and nuance really shine through.

Edward Burger

Dragon Games

It is fortunate that dragons don't live near where you do. They tend to like the wilder parts of the world, and whenever they happen upon a village, they make things very unpleasant for the people who live there, whether it's in the Himalayas, in Patagonia, or in the mountains of the East African Rift. Dragons have a big appetite for beautiful things made by clever human hands—their paws are too clumsy to create anything. If they see something beautiful, shiny, or brilliantly inventive, they simply must steal it. And they are so big and scary that no one except the most heroic men and women try to stop them.

Dragons make huge heaps of their stolen treasure and spend their time admiring it. With the tip of a giant claw they arrange gold coins and jewels into fancy patterns throughout their lair. You can do this too, and you can learn a lot about numbers when you do so.

Which Make Triangles?
Get a pile of pennies and start making triangles. Make some that have equal sides and some that are unequal. Make some that have one corner the same shape as the corner of this book (right angle). Is there a triangle that has two right angles?
Now build some solid triangles, that have the inside all filled in. If you do this neatly you'll see that you've made a pretty pattern. There's some pretty math here too, but I'll leave it up to your parent whether to introduce it to you or not.

Which Make Squares?
Get a handful of equally shaped and sized objects (circles work, but squares are best, so square cards, or the "one" unit of your number rods, etc.). Try to arrange them so they make a filled square.

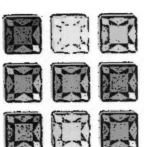

Which numbers make squares? Which don't? Why?

Why does adding up successive odd numbers (1+3+5+7) always make a square?

Can you see the relationship between triangle and square numbers? Maybe not so easily when you are looking at the number symbols, so model it. Draw a square on paper—how do you make two triangles out of it? Now make two triangles out of the square that you made with unit cubes. Then try it with a bigger square.

Now do you see the relationship between triangle and square numbers?

Magic Circles

The most magical shape of course is the circle—there is nothing more perfect than a perfect circle, and dragons love them. Anything can be turned into a circle if you spin it. Stretch a string between your hands— that's a straight line, right? But tie something to the end to give it weight and swing it over your head—now it's tracing out a circle! Take a small piece of paper of any shape, pin it to a bulletin board over a piece of cardstock, poke a pen through a corner of the shape and spin the shape.

You will have just drawn a circle. Circles are magically created out of anything!

Now cut out your circle and fold it in half, then cut along the line. Then take one of the halves and fold it in half and cut along that line, and then fold and cut again until you can't make it any smaller. Then cut another circle and fold it in half and then in thirds. Cut along three lines so that you have thirds, then fold one of them in half, and make sixths, and fold one in thirds and make ninths.

Can you put them in order from the largest to smallest pieces of a circle? The pointy end of the pieces is what we call an "angle"—not an angel, that's different. Angles can be wide open or almost shut. Draw a curved line across the tip and write what part of a circle it is: 1/2, 1/3, 1/4, etc.

Treasure hunt time! Take your angles and go find some that they match. Finding the 1/4 angle is easy, but for the others look at the patterns on furniture and fabric (quilts are great), toys and dishes, books and pictures. If you have pattern blocks, those will be good examples of your angles. Color your angles and fit them back together in attractive patterns the way a dragon would.

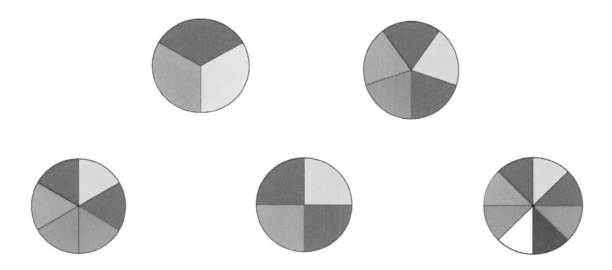

61

Perimeter and Area

In addition to pretty patterns to decorate their caves, dragons are always interested in better caves to put their treasure in. Big is great, but they also like the cave to have a lot of wall space to display their captured treasures. They can't build a cave for themselves, so they just have to go looking...and looking...and looking, like a fiddler crab searching for the perfect shell. In this way they get into a lot of trouble when they meet armed humans or other dragons.

Pretend you are a dragon in search of a cave with a lot of wall space for hanging tapestries and beautiful pieces of armor. Get some spaghetti and marshmallows, or some clay and toothpicks, or Wikistix® work great too. Try building a cube first, just to practice. A cube can be very large but doesn't have much wall space. So try making various different shapes for the base and then build up from there: triangles, hexagons, stars, etc. Think about what those shapes would be like if they were huge and you were inside them—which one would you want to live in if you liked LOTS of decorations on your walls?

Now get a bunch of papers—maybe 6 to 10 of them—and spread them on a table. Arrange them into a solid shape so that there is only an outside edge to the whole shape—with no gaps or holes inside. The area of a shape is how much ground it covers, like how many tiles you need to cover a floor. The perimeter (peri-around, meter-measure) is how much string you would need to go all the way around the edge of the shape. So do that! Get a piece of string and lay it around the entire shape, following all the edges closely. When you get back to where you started, cut the string. That's how long the perimeter of that shape is. Can you make a shape that has no overlaps or gaps that has a longer perimeter than the first one you made? Can you make one with a shorter perimeter?

LOGIC AND PLAY

Children build up a sense of their world through hands-on experimentation. Jean Piaget found that when young children were asked to judge the equivalence of two containers of liquid, they tended to overemphasize the height of the liquid and ignore its width. You could say, "If you're really thirsty, which glass of water would you like?" and show them a tall but very narrow glass and a slightly shorter but much wider one, and they would always choose the tall one. Piaget thought this reflected an inability to maintain and coordinate attention toward two dimensions at once. Children as old as seven have trouble understanding that when the same amount of food is divided among more plates, the size of the portions decrease, and this is simply because their brains are immature.

Interestingly, it has been shown that young children can perform logic problems beyond what is expected for their age as long as the problems are dressed up with silliness, fantasy, or humor. When they are fully engaged because it's interesting to them, and the threat of shame for being wrong is fully removed "because this is all in fun—just a game…" it appears that the brain can bring many more resources online for problem-solving.

Through play and experimenting with the real world, in the bathtub, the kitchen, the backyard, and the play room, children gradually eliminate wrong assumptions—which is one great reason to limit screen time: no matter how educational the game is, it's not the real world. Again, young children need physical objects to think with to form a solid number sense in the "concrete stage" of math brain development. Having this strong foundation will prevent their thinking from going too far astray once they are dealing with abstract math. Real math does live in the Land of Imagination, but we'll never take flight without a good runway.

Activity extensions:
Which Make Triangles
The simplest activities sometimes yield the most fascinating results. Triangle numbers are those obtained by adding together the successive integers (counting numbers), e.g. $1+2+3+4=10$. The figures they make are pretty, and in the sequence of triangle numbers, 1, 3, 6, 10, 15, 21, 28, 36, 45, 55, 66, 78, 91, 105, 120, 136, 153, 171…, we see one pattern jump out: odd, odd, even, even. So that's fun, but take it one step farther.
Each integer has a digital root, which is found by adding together the digits of the number. If the resulting number is a two digit number, then add those digits together again until you have a one digit number. For example, 28 is $2+8=10$, so then you add $1+0$ and get 1, which is the digital root of 28 (hint: this has nothing to do with square roots—completely different concept).

So pull out your pen and paper and find the digital roots of the triangle numbers—you'll like the pattern that emerges. Digital roots are like taking an X-ray of a number, to find out what's inside.

Which Make Squares

Over the course of teaching about math education I've been surprised by how many parents don't realize that square numbers are simply those that you can make an actual square out of. This is probably because schoolish math education goes straight to writing numbers on paper and never looks back (until 8th grade geometry, which reminds you that once upon a time you liked math…).

If you find the digital roots of the square numbers, you'll see a nice pattern forming as well—check this out by calculating digital roots for the first 15 or 20 square numbers. Now lay that pattern next to the sequence of multiples of 9 and you might catch onto something magical. For example, 7 x 7=49; adding those digits together gives you 13; adding those digits gives you 4. The difference between 49 and the multiple of 9 just smaller than 49—45—is exactly 4.
8 x 8 = 64; digital root is 1; 64 is 1 bigger than 63 (which is the closest smaller multiple of 9).
9 x 9 = 81; digital root is 9; 81 is 9 bigger than 72 (which is the closest smaller multiple of 9).

Try it, you'll like it. Do you show this to your bright eight-year-old? Perhaps, but reserve for the child the moment of discovery—let them have the "Ah-hah!" moment.

Circles and Angles

It isn't necessary to begin talking to young children about the 360 degrees of a circle—save that for when you learn about the Babylonians, who came up with that system. But thinking about circles and angles is natural for the observant child, or for any child who likes to make paper snowflakes correctly with six points. If their paper-folding and scissors skills are not very advanced, you may need to assist in making these angle manipulatives, but it's a trade-off between accuracy and a missed opportunity for hands-on learning.

Perimeter and Area

The purpose of these activities (like most in this book) is to get kids to start thinking about a new idea: ratios. Take square cards and have your child think about the following questions (use simple words, and demonstrate them) as he wraps the shapes that he's made out of the cards with a piece of string, then measures the string (use one side of the square for the measuring unit) and compares it to the number of cards.

"A square that's one unit wide has an area of one square unit and a perimeter of four units. When we want to think about these things together, we create a ratio: one square unit to four units of length; a ratio of 1:4. Does a square that's two units wide (four unit squares) maintain the same ratio? Why or why not? What if you take those same four squares and put them all in a line: what is the area:perimeter ratio then?"

Make several different shapes out of the same number of cards (like 4, or 9), and compare the findings. If you have the game Blockus®, now would be a good time to get it out and look at all the shapes you can make with three squares, four squares, and five squares. Which shapes have the most "edge" for the amount of "ground" that they cover? And how can understanding this help you win Blockus®?

Young children will probably not fully "get it" that a square with an area:perimeter ratio of 1:4 is a different beast* than the next unit square, which has an area:perimeter of 4:8, or the next one that has a ratio of 9:12, etc. The thinking may get a boost while contemplating the 4x4 square, which has an area:perimeter ratio of 16:16, but you have an adult brain, and that's a different matter. You could point out that the numbers are getting closer together in terms of "how much the first one IS of the second one." But remember that explanations often cause more confusion than they eliminate, and that's not really the point of the activity. The point is to get children thinking about these topics, since this begins building up the neural pathways required to, someday, have that "Aha!" moment on their own, which is when they really own it.

* Just between the two of us, and speaking of beasts, did you know that this concept relates to the maximum size of living creatures, and perhaps to why the dinosaurs went extinct? Of course, in dinosaurs it is surface area to volume ratios. Look it up!

Mathematics is a wonderful, mad subject, full of imagination, fantasy, and creativity that is not limited by the petty details of the physical world, but only by the strength of our inner light.

Gregory Chaitin

naiads, Dryads and symmetry

In the magical world there is much beauty and much danger, but for this last section let's talk about the beauty. People have long been fascinated by catching glimpses of naiads and dryads. Dryads are tree spirits who take the form of fair maidens and sometimes are willing to show themselves to humans and talk with them. Naiads are water spirits, and each one presides over a given lake or stream. They are even more shy than the dryads, and if you walk by a pond and see sudden ripples, it may be that a frog has just leaped into the water. Or you may have just disturbed a naiad.

Both naiads and dryads are very beautiful, and very vain. Narcissus, the son of a naiad, once saw his reflection in a stream and found himself so handsome that he couldn't stop admiring himself, so the silly boy starved. That is why you may find the narcissus flower growing at the edge of a pond, bending over to look at itself in the water.

But YOU know that beauty is only skin deep, and you'd rather be smart, right? So go look in a large mirror—I'm not worried that you'll stop eating. Look very carefully at how the image in the mirror changes as you walk past it. Now move up and down—what is being reflected when you are looking up into the mirror?

With your parent's permission, get a very small bouncy ball. Stand directly in front of the mirror and throw the ball at the reflection of your nose. Because of gravity, it won't bounce back and hit your nose, but should hit you right in the center of your body—straight on if you threw it from a place right in front of your nose.

Now stand to the side of the mirror and look at something reflected in the mirror—is there something on the wall behind you that you can take aim at, that is not too far away? Perhaps you can play a game where another person holds up an object behind you, and you try to hit it with the ball. Throw the ball directly at where you see the object on the mirror. Magic! If you throw straight from the center of your body, it should hit very close to where you aimed.

THINK about what is going on—why this works. You may want to keep playing with mirrors as you think. Use a mirror to look around corners in your home (but it's not nice to spy on people). On a sunny day, place the mirror in a pool of sunshine on the floor and move it around bouncing the light all over the room (be careful not to bounce light in someone's eyes).

But what does all this have to do with math? Just like the ball, light bounces off the mirror at the same angle that it travelled toward it. If you were to draw the path of the light that shows where it came from and where it went, then fold it in half, you would see that the

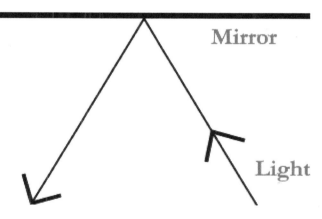

Mirror

Light

rays of light match up. Symmetry is the word for this, and symmetry is everywhere in science, in nature, and in math. Remember that math is all about patterns and making order out of chaos. So let's look at some types of symmetry.

Grab a small mirror and some books, alphabet blocks, or an alphabet puzzle: anything that has large plain letters printed on it. Put your mirror on the letter A and watch the reflection. Can you place the mirror somewhere on the A that makes it so that half of the real letter plus the reflection together look like a letter A? If you place the mirror vertically down the center of the A it will look correct, because A has vertical (up and down) symmetry.

NAIAD

Now find a capital B. Where can you place your mirror so that you can still see a B correctly? B has horizontal symmetry (the horizon is where the edge of the earth appears to meet the sky—that's how you can remember what that word means). Keep doing this with all the letters. You will see that with some of them you cannot put the mirror anywhere that will make the letter look right. Some of them have both horizontal and vertical symmetry. X also has diagonal symmetry, and O does too if it's a perfect circle.

But what about N? It doesn't seem to have symmetry—you can't reflect it correctly with a mirror. But there is another kind of symmetry that works here—rotational symmetry. Put your finger in the center of the N and rotate it half way around in a circle. Does it look the same as before?

What other letters have rotational symmetry?

What symmetry can you find in the numbers?

Can you find any short words that have horizontal or vertical symmetry?

Look for symmetry on your face. On an insect, a flower, a leaf, a tree. On the furniture in your home, on a flag, on a pinwheel. Everywhere you go you will find symmetry.

There are several other kinds of symmetry for you to discover, but one that relates to our topic of naiads and dryads, water spirits and tree spirits, is expanding symmetry, or fractals. When the dryads are in tree form, they have beautiful expanding symmetry.

Have you ever, while creating a tiny doll village in your garden or sandbox, plucked the tip of a branch from a tree and stuck it in the ground to be a shade tree for a doll's house? If so, you noticed that the tree branch looks a lot like a small copy of the real tree. Most living thing are like that—they grow by creating tiny copies of themselves which then grow big and create tiny copies of themselves. There is a lot of math in this principle, so let's do some.

Draw a vertical line on a piece of paper (or in the sand if you're outside making a doll village with shade trees). At the top of the line, make it branch—draw two lines, each <u>half the length</u> of your first line, so it looks like the letter Y. Now at the end of each of those branches, make two more branches, each half the length of your second lines; now you have four branch tips, out of which sprout two more at half the length of the previous ones. Continue this pattern. Eventually you'll have a very crowded picture, so stop.

One interesting thing about your fractal tree is that if, before you start adding branches, you draw a circle around your tree that is twice as big as your tree is tall, with the top of your tree in the center of the circle, then add branches according to our rule, each half the length of the previous one, you will never ever ever ever ever reach the circle with the branch tips. Don't believe me? Try it—but you must be very precise.

Guess what? You just did some calculus, which is math that describes the living, changing, moving world that we live in.

Now pretend that you're an ant. When the tree was just one straight stick, crawling up one side and down the other would mean that you have travelled two tree lengths—we'll call them units. When you add the branches, each branch is half a unit long, so going up and down it is one unit. So you've just added 2 more units for you (as an ant) to crawl in your trip all the way around this tree. When you add 2 more branches to each of the first 2, those are each ¼ of the length of the first tree, so the ant has to crawl ½ unit to get around them, and you've drawn 4, so you've again added 2 units to the length the ant must crawl to get back to the ground on the other side of the tree.

See if this pattern continues as you add 8 branches that are 1/8th as long as your first tree, but have two sides to travel. Each time new branches grow, does the ant only have to travel 2 extra units? Really? Even when you add 1024 branches (on the tenth level of branching)—he just goes 2 more units?

What if you had a powerful magnifying glass, and you zoomed into the tree tips and kept adding ever tinier branches? And when that got crowded you zoomed in again and added more, and again and again? If you did this forever you'd have created a line that was infinitely long; the ant could walk around the tree forever but never get to the other side. All within the circle that you drew in the beginning. Go figure!

Reflecting Reflections

Back to the naiads, who love to see their reflection in pools of water. Do you have a hinged mirror? Or two hand mirrors with very narrow frames (wide frames mess this up) that you can tape together? Or you can cut out two pieces of shiny mylar and tape them onto a folded piece of cardboard.

Place a small toy in front of the mirrors. When the mirror are open flat, in a straight line, you should see just two of your toy: the real one, and its reflection. Now start folding the mirrors. When can you see three toys? Four? When can you can see the most toys?

Now remember those circles that you drew and cut into pieces for the dragon games? Run and grab them. Place your mirrors so it looks like there are four toys instead of one. Now look at your circle pieces—which one would fit in between the mirrors? Play around with this, and notice what happens to the image when you put each different circle fraction in between the mirrors.

Next try placing the mirrors so that a straight line runs under both of them when slightly folded. Then fold the mirrors to different angles. What shapes are you creating?

Do you have pattern blocks with triangles, squares, hexagons and such? If you don't, you should ask for them on your next birthday—so much fun! If you do, pull them out and play with them. Which ones can be reflected to create a hexagon? Which cannot? Why?

Create beautiful flowers by making a pattern and reflecting it many times with your hinged mirrors. This may lead you into a study of which real flowers have petals in multiples of three, and which have multiples of four or five... which can lead you into the study of Fibonacci numbers and the golden ratio... which can lead you anywhere.

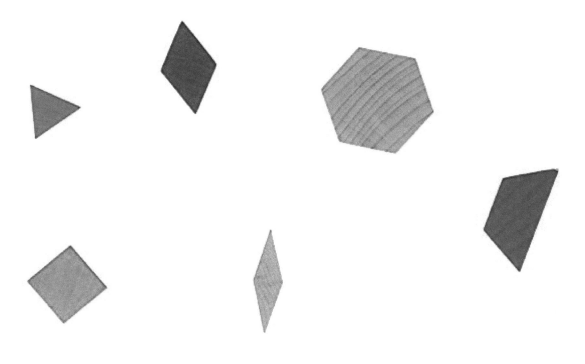

The Big Picture

For decades there has been a battle raging between math educators who believe in teaching concepts and those who believe in teaching calculations—the former being seen as reformist education and the latter being seen as traditional or even classical education. But if we reach all the way back to classical times, we see that the ancients viewed math as a journey of discovery. Calculations were fine for the masses: for the merchants dealing with weights and measures and the builders dealing with constructing a pyramid. But the educated classes studied the properties of a circle and the square root of two. They spent time thinking about the big picture of math, and this made them smarter. Advances in mathematics were then possible.

One reason to help children focus on building thinking skills instead of just memorizing calculations is that math is a work in progress; we are still discovering math. As Jordan Ellenberg states, "Mathematics is not settled. Even concerning the basic objects of study, like numbers and geometric figures, our ignorance is much greater than our knowledge. And the things we do know were arrived at only after massive effort, contention, and confusion. All this sweat and tumult is carefully screened off in your textbook."

This wide-ranging view of what mathematics is for and about cannot obviously be presented to children all at once. But the least we can do is to not kill a dawning interest in math by beating it over the head with arithmetic problems. Instead, we should nurture this new magical creature by feeding it simple ideas that have deep roots, by providing mathematical tools and encouraging their use, by spending time with our child engaged in mathematical pursuits in the form of games and activities.

In his book *The Psychology of Learning Mathematics*, Richard Skemp says, "Mathematics is the most abstract, and so the most powerful of all theoretical system…. Its usefulness is, however, only potential, and many who work wearily at trying to learn it throughout their schooldays derive little benefit, and no enjoyment. This is almost certainly because they are not really learning mathematics at all….What is inflicted on all too many children and older students is the manipulation of symbols with little or no meaning attached, according to a number of rote-memorized rules. This is not only boring (because meaningless); it is very much harder, because unconnected rules are much harder to remember than an integrated conceptual structure."

So children need to understand math concepts, but do they also need to learn to calculate? Yes, certainly, and they will. If you take just one thing away from this book, let it be this: math facts and abstract rules should be memorized only when the individual child is ready.

And she is ready after she's spent a lot of time thinking with her hands, ears, eyes, and mouth—all appendages of her brain—discovering the structure of the mathematical world. At that point, learning facts and rules will be cake, since she'll have a "gut instinct" about what the answer should be. The long division mantra "divide, multiply, subtract, bring down" won't be just arbitrary steps, but will be natural and logical.

Let's focus in closing on a principle very well-stated in the aforementioned book:

> **Mathematics, like music, needs to be expressed in physical actions and human interactions before its symbols can evoke the silent patterns of mathematical ideas (like musical notes), simultaneous relationships (like harmonies), and expositions or proofs (like melodies).**
>
> *Richard Skemp*

There is no substitute for physical actions and human interactions, especially for young children. Handing a child a boring math workbook and telling her to go do some of it is a recipe for creating a math-hater. No amount of clip art on pages of arithmetic problems will make that workbook interesting. What your child needs are physical objects to move around, and an engaged parent who will listen and respond as she talks about what she's doing. If you create a family culture where math is valued as an interesting and useful endeavor—a conversation-starter at the dinner table—you will certainly be successful in raising a child who has a healthy relationship with math.

Quote References ❝❞ Further Reading ❓ and Fun Stuff

5   ❝❞   Chesterton, G.K. 1935. *The Scandal of Father Brown* - "The Point of a Pin." London: Cassel & Co.

9   ❝❞   Holt, John Caldwell. 1989. *Learning All The Time* - 53. Cambridge, Massachusetts: Perseus Publishing.

13   ❝❞   Rogers, Fred. 2003. *The World According to Mister Rogers*

17   ❝❞   Beechick, Ruth. 1999. *You CAN Teach Your Child Successfully* - 205. Michigan: Mott Media.

21   ❝❞   Descartes, René. 1637. *Discourse on the Method of Rightly Conducting One's Reason and of Seeking Truth in the Sciences*

24   ❓   Vygotsky, Lev S. 1978. *Mind in Society: Development of Higher Psychological Processes*

     ❓   "brain-mind cycle of reflection" Bransford et al., *How People Learn: Brain, Mind, Experience, and School*

25   ❝❞   Einstein, Albert. 1947. Cited as conversation between Einstein and János Plesch in *János : The Story of a Doctor*, by János Plesch

29   ❝❞   Scarfe, N.V. 1962. *Play is Education*

32   ❝❞   Miendlarzewska, Ewa and Wiebke J. Trost. 2013. "How musical training affects cognitive development: rhythm, reward and other modulating variables" *Frontiers in Neuroscience* 2013; 7: 279. Accessed Feb. 24, 2017. doi:10.3389/fnins.2013.00279

33   ❝❞   Hardy, G.H. 1940. *A Mathematician's Apology*

37   ❝❞   What's in a Number?© game available at visionacademypublishing.com

     ❝❞   Fun websites: gwydir.demon.co.uk/jo/mathsindex.htm, mathisfun.com, cut-the-knot.org

37   datapointed.net/visualizations/math/factorization/animated-diagrams/

mathworld.wolfram.com

Bellos, Alex. 2014. *The Grapes of Math: How Life Reflects Numbers and Numbers Reflect Life*. New York: Simon & Schuster

Pólya, George. 1962. *Mathematical Discovery: On Understanding, Learning and Teaching Problem Solving*

41   Holt, John. 1983. *How Children Learn* - 221, Cambridge, Massachusetts: Perseus Publishing.

44   Montessori, Maria. 1936. *The Secret of Childhood*

Mason, Charlotte. 1905. *Home Education Series*

Gray, Peter. 2013. *Free to Learn : Why unleashing the instinct to play will make our children happier, more self-reliant, and better students for life*

45   Aristotle. *Metaphysics* 982a16

50   Gardner, Howard (1983; 1993) F*rames of Mind: The theory of multiple intelligences*

51   Sanchez, Dan. 2016. "Spark and Fuel: How to Help your Child Learn Without Resorting to Compulsion." Foundation for Economic Education. https://fee.org/articles/spark-and-fuel-how-to-help-your-child-learn-without-resorting-to-compulsion/

54   If you'd like a demonstration of this activity, do a search for Vi Hart's video "Doodling in Math: Stars," which you can find on Khan Academy or on her own website. And if you want a demonstration with even more sassiness and humor, check out "Doodling in Math: Connecting Dots."

55   http://www.ernweb.com/educational-research-articles/mathematics-teaching-in-japan/

57   Burger, Edward. 2003. *The Joy of Thinking and the Beauty and Power of Classical Mathematical Ideas*. The Great Courses

64 ? Dias, M.G. and Harris, P. L. "The influence of imagination on reasoning by young children." *The British Journal of Developmental Psychology*, November 1990

65   mathisfun.com/games

67   Chaitin, Gregory. "Less Proof, More Truth". Review of *How Mathematicians Think*, by William Byers, *New Scientist*, July 28, 2007.

73   Look up the tree fractal generator on scratch.mit.edu

73   http://www.maths.surrey.ac.uk/hosted-sites/R.Knott/Fibonacci/fibnat.html

76   Ellenberg, Jordan. 2014. *How Not To Be Wrong: The Power of Mathematical Thinking*. New York: Penguin.

77   Skemp, Richard. 1987. *The Psychology of Learning Mathematics*. New York: Taylor and Francis.

 ? An interesting article summarizing some studies of the effects of direct instruction on early childhood development is at slate.com/articles/double_x/doublex/2011/03/why_preschool_shouldnt_be_like_school

notes

Jennifer Georgia has been loving math since the moment fifteen years ago when she rebelled against the "schoolish math" that she'd been using in her homeschool and embraced math as the fascinating creature that it is. Since that time her focus has been finding ways to spread a feast of inherently-appealing math before her children and many others so that they gain a holistic view of what math is. She reads every book on math she can get her hands on, and teaches it to children in co-ops, classes, and tutoring sessions.

By profession Jennifer is a critical care nurse, but her career is motherhood. She and her husband Paul now have four homeschool graduates whose first day of "school" was in college, along with a kindergartener and three soon-to-be adopted foster children. She has been the chairman of a national homeschool organization and has been a speaker at many homeschool conferences. The Georgias live in northern Virginia outside of Washington D.C.

Adrianne, Quinn, and Luke Georgia have been creating artwork since they were tiny. As homeschool kids they had plenty of time to follow their passions, and this is one of the biggest. Adrianne prefers character art created on a computer, Quinn dabbles in several art media and styles, and Luke loves to make pen and ink sketches of ghastly creatures. The Georgia kids grew up in Virginia and have now all launched into adulthood with college and jobs and such things.

At Vision Academy Publishing, our mission is to create high-quality materials for educating young people and their parents. We hope to inspire people to learn beautiful things and become a force for good in society. We believe that every person has unique gifts, and that one-size-fits-all education is inferior to a model which respects and supports the learner.

Look for more products coming soon: *Mystical Math: A book for older children and their parents*— a journey around the world and through time exploring fascinating math concepts and their historical connections.
Marvellous Math: An open-exploration book for teens—activities, games, and thought-provoking ideas to encourage teens to look beyond traditional math topics.

CPSIA information can be obtained
at www.ICGtesting.com
Printed in the USA
LVHW071319291119
638940LV00016B/877/P